Our house is a safe house

Photography by Bill Thomas

We have a safe house.

3

The kitchen

We stay away
from the stove.
The stove can get very hot.
We stay away
from the hot water, too.

We do not run in this room.

The bathroom

Mom and Dad keep us
away from the hot water.

The **cold** water
goes into the tub first.

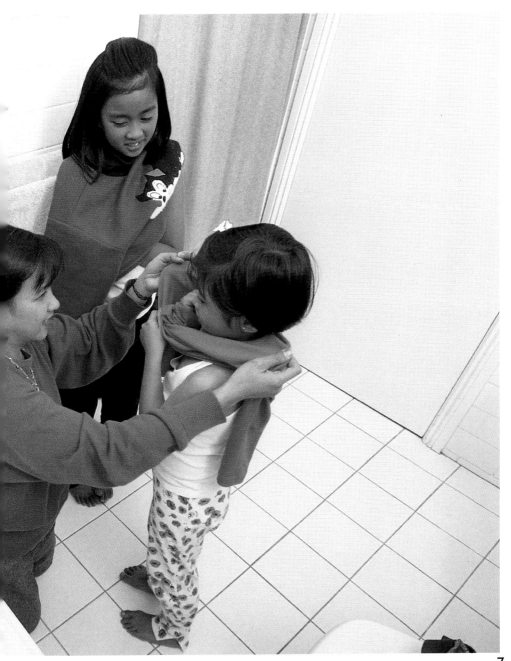

7

The family room

The heater is by the wall.

Mom and Dad do not let us
play by it.

We play with our toys
in a safe place.

9

The bedroom

We sleep in here,
and we play here, too.

This big box is for our toys.

The shed

We have a shed at our house.
It has a lock on the door.

Mom and Dad do not let us
play in the shed.

We help to look after
our little brother.

He is safe in his playpen.

He is safe
in his chair.

He is safe in his bed, too.

We all help to make
our house a safe place.